A DEVOTIONAL

Jottings on the Journey

ANITA BACKMAN

Ark House Press
arkhousepress.com

Cataloguing in Publication Data:
Title: Jottings on the Journey
ISBN: 978-1-7640298-7-2 (pbk)
Subjects: REL012170   RELIGION / Christian Living / Personal Memoirs; POE023080 POETRY / Subjects & Themes / Motivational & Inspirational;
Design by initiateagency.com

Table of Contents

I Mustn't Ponder Too Long

The sky explodes with colour. Golden yellow light. It's a new day, and I know how important sunrise is to my mother.

You see, I am only a little dog … a Moodle named Hugo. Cheeky, spontaneously playful; a handsome chap that always turns heads on morning walks. Little do people know the pain and suffering my mother goes through day and night.

This coastal holiday on the rocks on Merimbula Beach gives me time to contemplate our lives.

We are one, mum and I. Loyalty is my biggest pride. Mum is quite sick. She suffers from bipolar mood disorder, complex PTSD and chronic pain. These illnesses plague her, but she does a mighty job in getting on with life.

The nights are often long, lonely and sleepless. When nightmares take place, it's my job to rescue her. I jump off the bed and bark at her. She awakes with the light on. I bark at her to get out of bed and go to the door. I jump downstairs slowly, making sure she is following. I sit at the fridge and mum has a drink. Then I fly back upstairs and it's back to bed for both of us. My night watch job is complete.

Each morning, I jump on mum's chest, licks all over her cheeks. A big long pat, a belly rub and a kiss on the forehead starts our day. Some days are slow going, where the pain is so bad mum uses a walking stick, and we only stroll for 10 minutes. These days I know not to pull on the lead, but rather walk right at her feet. This is my way of showing I care as I slow down and relax into her pace. Other days we are like a bull at a gate. I pull, sniff, do a hundred phantom wees and we enjoy the pleasure of movement.

When mum is manic, I must admit I do find it a little hard. She talks to me all the time and is agitated. This in turn wires me up, but I try hard not to let it, because she needs calm. The days when mum suffers depression are not pleasant, either. I snuggle up to her, lick the tears from her cheeks, and provide much needed love and understanding.

So, it's another coastal holiday trip. Mum and I always have a blast! This sunrise, however, has me a little concerned, quite worried to be honest … I'm getting older now. What will mum do without me when it's my time?

The sun glows a brilliant yellow. The ocean waves hit the rocks. I mustn't ponder on this question for too long.

Written in 2023. Hugo very sadly went to sleep in July 2024 at 11 years of age. Thank you God for such a wonderful, loving, loyal and cheeky mate whom you blessed me with to help get through so many trials.

❧

"Lord, direct me throughout my journey so I can experience your plans for my life. Reveal the life-paths that are pleasing to you.

"Escort me along the way; take me by the hand and teach me. For you are the God of my increasing salvation; I have my heart wrapped into yours!"

Psalm 25:2-5 TPT

❧

Introduction

Hello,

Welcome to *Jottings on the Journey*.

Let me ask you a question …

What does the word 'journey' mean to you? How does the word 'journey' impact your experience of life, if at all?

For me, the word journey is a lifetime living with God. It is a comfy pillow when I'm stuck in bed with chronic pain, yet still able to enjoy sunrise through my widow. It is the highs and lows of living with bipolar – the dark depression needing moments of wailing and comfort, the mania where my racing mind needs peace. The care of nurses when I am in a mental health unit for recovery. It is the refuge God provides from flashbacks of complex post-traumatic stress disorder.

It is a journey of conversation; talking to God all the time, everywhere and being in tune with His voice through nature, people, music, creativity and scripture. It is not easy. At times, it is downright hard. However, it is beautiful … an intimate relationship with the one who loves me the most.

Would you like to join me in exploring the journey with God?

This book covers an array of topics. With each written piece, there are questions and a space to jot your journey. These jottings can be a word, a drawing, a scripture verse or short story… anything that is on your heart. Just jot it down. Why? Because it's your journey, one of self-discovery while walking with God and deepening your relationship with Him.

So, I would like to invite you to turn the page and journey with me, as a friend and child of God … Let's journey and jot together.

Blessings, *Anita*

Who is in charge of your journey?

"We make our plans, but the Lord determines our steps." Proverbs 16:9 NLT

God is all that we have. He is in charge of our journey, and the only thing that will last and endure is the word he speaks into our hearts, which allows us to have a strong faith.

We all have to go through 'things', and in difficult circumstances, it is hard not to spend time asking 'why' is this happening, and 'when' will it end?

Our first chat with God in these circumstances should be, 'God, please help me.'

It's hard to represent God in your difficult times, especially when others look like they have blessings overflowing from their lives because they are in a good season. Sometimes God puts off, or withholds what we are pleading for because he wants us to go deeper within Him. He wants us to yearn for Him; for our inner souls to be full of faith, love and peace . He wants us to "seek first the kingdom of God."

By seeking God's face, we are able to keep God's commands when we feel we are in the desert. God is in charge of our journey, and sometimes difficult circumstances are to test us so we become more dependent on God and develop a more intimate relationship with him. This in turn is a real blessing within its self because without God, we are nothing. But in God we are everything.

Is God in charge of your journey, or are you sidetracked with more superficial things like money or success? Jot your thoughts.

Prayers

What is on your heart?
What do you want to chat to God about?

Use this space to chat with God in any way
– drawing, scripture, writing.

It does not need to be neat and perfect, actually the
messier the better. Just pour out your heart to him.

A Prayer to be Entwined with Jesus

Jesus,

Draw me closer to you.

My heart wants nothing more than to be in sync with yours,
My eyes want to gaze reverently at your scars.
My ears want to hear the promises of your word.
My lips want to praise you in songs of delight,
As my arms reach out to hold you tight.

I want your Holy Spirit to invade me.
I want your will done for my life.
I want to honour you in all I say and do,
And I want to testify your greatness in my life.

I want you to shine through me,
Even in the darkness of deep depression …
I want to be a light,
A beacon of your love;
A treasure chest showcasing your
Might, your glory, your hope, peace and strength!

For I am yours,
And you are mine,
This is where I belong …

With you
Worshipping you
Loving you.

Together we are entwined.

"The [reverent] fear of the LORD [that is, worshipping Him and regarding Him as truly awesome] is the beginning and the preeminent part of wisdom [its starting point and its essence], And the knowledge of the Holy One is understanding and spiritual insight."
Proverbs 9:10 AMP

. . . . . .

Jottings

Write a prayer or draw a picture about your connection with Jesus at this very moment.

What does it feel like? Are you close or distant?

A Fresh Start Every Day

God,
It is a new day.
The sun is rising.
And a bright yellow glow lights up the sky …

Yesterday,
I may have said or done things that were not of you.
I may have offended someone,
Not listened properly
Became impatient
Got angry.

It is a fresh start today,
And I ask for your forgiveness for any wrong-doings yesterday.
Because you are the God of love,
The slate has been wiped clean.

Today,
I ask that you may help me God,
To live within your Kingdom
In a way that honours you,
And honours others.

As the sky lights up,
Let my heart shine with your goodness.

If I slip up today,
Gently bring my heart under conviction,
And guide me on the right path for this day.

For today is a fresh start,
And for that I am grateful.

> *"Teach me more about you, how you work and how you move, so that I can walk onward in your truth until everything within me brings honour to your name."*
> *Psalm 86:11 TPT*

. . . . . .

Jottings

What do you need for this new day?
Ask God for his guidance in truth.

A Sunset Prayer

Lord,

As the day draws to a close, I want to take this opportunity to just be with you in gratitude … to be resting in your arms, my head on your shoulder, your love wrapped around me. My lungs gently rising and falling, breathing in your life. My ears open to the whisper of your voice, telling me I am secure in your love, and my eyes softly gazing into yours … My compassionate Father.

"So I have gazed upon you in the sanctuary, to see Your power and Your glory. Because Your loving kindness is better than life, my lips shall praise You."
Psalm 63:2-3 MSG

. . . . . .

Jottings

You are sitting in Gods arms this very minute.
How does it feel?
What would you like to say to Him?
Take a moment to listen to his voice whispering in your ear.
Draw or write your response.

A Night Time Prayer

Lord,

I pray that as I go to sleep,
Down from heaven you will kiss my cheek.
Please cuddle me with your love
Washing peace over me from heaven above.

Throughout the night
Be by my side
Wrap me in your warmth,
And smile on me through the moonlight.

May my dreams be filled
With the goodness of your love.
Thanking you for abundant blessings
Brought to me by the death of your Son.

And as morning approaches,
Wake me gently …
Let me savour the night of deep rest.
Then,
Let me sing with the chirping birds
For all the good things in this day that you have promised

> *"You can go to bed without fear; you will lie down and sleep soundly."*
> *Proverbs 3:24 NLT*

Jottings

Does anything of the night scare or worry you?
Bring these fears and worries to our loving, protective Father.

Infuse

Sitting here in your presence, I invite you to come into the depths of my heart and mind. Come and infuse me with your light and love ... touch every part of my life.

I sit here in surrender.

Flood me with your Spirit. Overwhelm me with love, peace and joy. Fill all the cracks in my heart and mind with your hope and grace.

Let your light shine brightly, a path for my feet, as I am a pilgrim on a journey.

Warm my heart with your love, refresh my soul. Let me radiate your brilliance to the world around me. Fill me up to overflow.

> *"Breathtaking brilliance and awe-inspiring majesty radiate from his shining presence. His stunning beauty overwhelms all who come before him."*
> *Psalm 96:6 TPT*

Jottings

Invite God into your heart and mind.
Tell him about any darkness you may be experiencing.
Give it to God in surrender.
Ask God to infuse you with his luminous light, making your
path shine bright and your heart glowing to the world.

A Prayer to Remember God's help

Lord,

I have become increasingly aware that I am turning inwards to my own strength and problem-solving skills to try and resolve the problems I am facing. This is not helping me. It is making my heart cold and stubborn, and my worries are getting bigger.

Let me not forget, Lord, that you want to help me. All I need to do is call on your name and you will come running. Then, Lord, help me to be observant of the movings of the Holy Spirit so I can rest safe and secure in your loving arms, as you help me overcome my problems through your strength.

Amen.

> *"For the same God who made everything, our Creator and mighty maker, he himself is our helper and defender."*
> *Psalm 124:8 TPT*

Jottings

What battles and struggles are you trying to face on your own?
Is this helping or hindering you?
Do you need to ask God for help? If so, write down
your prayer request to our mighty God.

Shedding Bark

Dear God,

Eucalyptus trees shed their bark so they can grow. The bark falls and sits at the base of the tree. The trunk of the tree grows new bark that is often coloured and slowly fades with time, repeating the whole process each year.

Today, I boldly ask you to shed my bark so I can grow. Shed everything in me that is impure: unforgiveness, jealously, impatience, anger – let it fall and sit at the foot of your cross.

Allow me to grow new bark; the colourful bark of the Fruits of the Spirit – love, joy, peace, patience, kindness, goodness, faithfulness, gentleness and self-control.

When my growth becomes stunted because my bark has again become impure, I ask you to repeat the process of shedding my bark and placing it at the foot of your cross so I can continue to grow.

> *"So get rid of your old self, which made you live as you used to – the old self that was being destroyed by deceitful desires. Your hearts and minds must be made completely new, and you must put on the new self, which is created in God's likeness and reveals itself in the true life that is upright and holy."*
> *Ephesians 4:22-24 GNT*

Jottings

What bark do you want to shed and leave at the foot of the cross?

A Prayer for Unwavering Faith

Lord,

I pray for unwavering faith.

As constant and reliable as the sunrise and sunset each day, so is the truth of your word. It is unchanging.

When doubts cloud my mind, reveal your closeness, and fill me with the promise of your truth.

Make my faith bold and great! In all circumstances, let me trust your ways. Amen.

> *"Jesus responded, 'If you have even the smallest measure of authentic faith, it would be powerful enough to say to this large tree, 'My faith will pull you up by the roots and throw you into the sea,' and it will respond to your faith and obey you.'"*
> *Luke 17:16 TPT*

Jottings

What doubts cloud your mind?
Ask God to fill these doubts with faith and trust.
Invite him into your circumstances.

A Prayer for the Tired Pilgrim

Lavish your love upon me, God, for my soul is dry. Awaken my heart, bring it to life … warm it with hope and peace.

Open my eyes to see your glorious face. A face of radiant majesty where I can gaze at you in adoration.

Hold my hands. Infuse me with your mighty strength.

Alert my ears to the whispers of your voice and the calling on my life.

Allow my mouth to speak of your goodness, my lips to sing you songs of praise.

And,

Guide my footsteps so I do not stray, but walk on the path you have already prepared for me.
Amen.

> *"So be made strong even in your weakness by lifting up your tired hands in prayer and worship. And strengthen your weak knees, for as you keep walking forward on God's path all your stumbling ways will be divinely healed!"*
> *Hebrews 12:12-13 TPT*

Jottings

Are you tired?
Do you feel spiritually dry?
Take some time to explain to God how you feel … don't hold back.
Ask God to revitalize your heart and mind.

A Prayer for the Hurting

I want to know your heart, for I am lost and numb.
I want to feel your love beat inside my chest, for I feel disconnected.

I want to know forgiveness, for I am a sinner.
I want to know your peace, for I am rippled with anxiety.

I want to know compassion, for I cannot show it to myself.

I want to know you, Jesus, for you bring light and life.

Jesus, although I am afflicted at this point in time, I know you are faithful.
I look back on my life and I see your hand on every season. This again is
a season of distress. I cry out to you, and I know you hear me. You are a
faithful, loving God, and I know you will deliver me.

> *"I'm hurt and in pain: Give me space for healing and mountain air."*
> *Psalm 69:29 MSG*

Jottings

Are you hurting?
Are you lost or disconnected?
What are you like at showing yourself 'self-compassion?'
Tell God about it. He has big ears so don't hold back!

Dusting off the Lightbulb

Not wanting to live in the dark anymore, I've dusted off the lightbulb and have decided I don't want to be on dimmer any longer. So, I've hit the switch – bright electricity running through my heart on full time glow as I want to shine for you, Jesus.

I want to be an example, to be a constant witness to You, my Lord, to fulfill your assignment for my life, as your Good News, healing and blessings I am called to share with all.

I am your seed, and you have me planted right where you need me to be. I've got my own sphere of influence, where people can see I'm living for you, with the bright light bulb of you, My Lord, shining inside of me.

> *"You are the light of the world – like a city on a hill top that cannot be hidden. No one lights a lamp then puts it under a basket. Instead, a lamp is placed on a stand, where it gives light to everyone in the house. In the same way, let your good deeds shine out for all to see, so that everyone will see your heavenly Father."*
> *Matthew 5:14-16 NLT*

Jottings

Do you want to shine for Jesus?
How can you do this with your own sphere of influence?

Illuminate

Loving Father,

We all fall into patches of darkness at times where we cannot see. We walk around bumping into things, bruising ourselves because we are blinded by darkness.

Come and shine on us Lord! Illuminate our paths so we can walk with you in your glorious light.

Guide our every step in your wisdom as to where we walk on our journey. If we go astray, lead us back by the brilliance of your light, keeping us from the shadows of darkness.
Amen.

> *"God all at once you turned on a floodlight for me! You are the revelation light in my darkness, and in your brightness I can see the path ahead."*
> *Psalm 18:28 TPT*

Jottings

In this moment, what do you need God to light up, to illuminate for you, so you can see?

The Potter Sits at His Wheel Moulding Clay

Loving Father,

Each one of us is unique and gifted, filled with your Spirit that breathes life into us. Like a potter sitting at his wheel moulding clay, you mould us, you form us, you shape us into what you want us to be.

Sometimes life circumstances and situations can change us, and it is possible for your perfect moulding to go pear-shaped in our eyes.

Although we are imperfect people, and at times the clay becomes dry and cracks, it must be remembered that you, God, moulded us perfect in your eyes.

Your potter's wheel allows us to be continually shaped and open to your transformation of our hearts and minds. This is because ultimately, you are the graceful potter and we are the supple clay.
Amen.

> *"And yet, O Lord, you are our Father. We are the clay and you are the potter. We are all formed by your hand."*
> *Isaiah 64:8 NLT*

Jottings

*What situations and circumstances have changed
you to make you cracked and dry?
Are you aware that you are being continually shaped by God? If
so, how? If not, ask God to show you his transformative power.*

Reflections

Think about your life over the last few months.
What have your learnt?
How have you grown?
Take some time to reflect on these things and jot them down.

Sin, Drought, Surrender, Forgiveness, Freedom

What season are you living in…? A study of Psalm 32:1-5

Has there ever been a time in your life when sin has greatly affected the way you live?

Maybe anger, hatred, or jealousy has taken hold of your heart and it has affected your interactions with others, or even cut you off from other people.

Perhaps you have experienced a spiritual drought due to sin's hold on your heart and connecting with God has been difficult.

And it may even be possible that you don't know you are holding sin in your heart simply because that's the way it has always been.

In my journey, life's hurts and ill health have led me into all five seasons of sin, drought, surrender, forgiveness and freedom.

I suffer with bipolar 1 mood disorder, C-PTSD (complex post-traumatic stress disorder), an eating disorder and anxiety, as well as chronic pain. I have also suffered abuse in many forms. With all this pain and trauma, I had a frozen heart. It was cold, thumping in my chest, and I could not feel God's presence. Sin had taken over my heart. Anger, hatred and jealously of other people's lives compared to mine completely crippled me, and I ended up in a spiritual drought, due to my sin.

So, my question is:

Do you need to confess any sin that is holding you back from an increasing interpersonal relationship with God, which is preventing you from living in the full freedom of Christ?

This is a big question. It is an uncomfortable question, and it is a hard question to answer.

Psalm 32:1-5 helped me to realise that I was holding sin in my heart; that I was in a spiritual drought, and that I needed to confess through surrender which brought, and still is bringing, forgiveness and freedom.

> *"How happy and fulfilled are those whose*
> *rebellion has been forgiven. How blessed*
> *and relieved are those who have confessed*
> *their corruption to God!*
>
> *"For he wipes their slates clean and*
> *removes hypocrisy from their hearts.*
> *"Before I confessed my sins, I kept it all inside;*
> *my dishonesty devastated my inner life,*
> *causing my life to be filled with frustration, irrepressible anguish*
> *and misery.*
>
> *"The pain never let up, for your hand*
> *of conviction was heavy on my heart.*
> *My strength was sapped, my inner life dried up like a spiritual*
> *drought within my soul.*
> *"Then, I finally admitted to you all my sins, refusing to hide them*
> *any longer.*
> *"So I said, "My life-giving God,*
> *I'll openly acknowledge my evil actions."*

And
you forgave me!
All at once the guilt of my sin washed away and
all my pain disappeared!"

So, let's break it down into five seasons:

1. **Sin**
2. **Spiritual drought**
3. **Surender**
4. **Forgiveness**
5. **Freedom**

Wikipedia has a few descriptions of sin. The description that resonated with me the most in my situation is this:

SIN – any thought or action that endangers the ideal relationship between the individual and God.

Bang, spot on! This is exactly how I felt. My anger, hatred and jealousy towards people in my life had completely crippled my heart and mind. David expresses it perfectly in Verse 3:

> *"Before I confessed my sins, I kept it all inside; my dishonesty devastated my inner life, causing my life to be filled with frustration, irrepressible anguish and misery."*

And that's what it felt like for me. I had suppressed things for a long time. The rage I had was 'just', and God showed me that as well. However, it was being played out in my life through episodes of self-harm.

All of this sin – the yuckiness, the thoughts, the self-harm, the anger, hatred and jealousy – brought me to a spiritual drought with my Heavenly Father.

This leads onto season two:
SPIRITUAL DROUGHT

Wikipedia explains spiritual dryness like this:

'It is a form of spiritual crisis experienced subjectively as a sense of separation from God or lack of spiritual feeling especially during contemplative prayer.'

This was so true for me. I could not feel God's presence and it was heart-wrenching. I was in denial that I was in sin. I thought that I was living through all the normal human emotions that would come up in such situations. Yes, they are all normal human emotions, and I had every right to feel each one of them. However, they had taken control of my life, which is not healthy. I couldn't read the bible or pray. I would listen to my praise and worship music, but it did nothing for me. Hearing from God was so hard, and not experiencing his presence was so difficult because I had never felt anything like this before.

In verse 4, David speaks about what being in spiritual dryness is like:

> *"The pain never let up, for your hand*
> *of conviction was heavy on my heart.*
> *My strength was sapped, my inner life dried up like a spiritual*
> *drought within my soul."*

I was dry, so dry. I had the hunger and thirst for God. All I could do was cry out to God in pure honesty of my feelings and situation. I poured out my heart to God…

This leads to season three:
SURRENDER

I surrendered every thought I had. I told God how angry I was with all the abuse. I told God that I was angry with the way my life was, with so much ill-health. I told God I was jealous of other people's lives. The relief was overwhelming. As David states in verse 5:

> *"Then, I finally admitted to you all my sins,*
> *refusing to hide them any longer.*
> *So I said, "My life-giving God,*
> *I'll openly acknowledge my evil actions." And*
> *you forgave me!*
> *All at once the guilt of my sin washed away and*
> *all my pain disappeared!"*

There was an important moment here - I needed to confess my sins in front of another and before God.

This leads to season four:
FORGIVENESS.

Now, **forgiveness is the action or process of forgiving or being forgiven**. I experienced both. I was asking God to forgive me for the sins I had towards the people who abused me, and the jealously of other people's lives. I asked for forgiveness from the anger I held about my ill-health. It was like a huge load had been lifted of my shoulders, my heart was back in sync with God's and I smiled for the first time in a long while.

With God having forgiven me, I asked God to soften my heart so that I could forgive others. I prayed a blessing over the people who abused me, and those who I was jealous of. To pray these blessings over the lives of others was quite freeing.

This leads to season five:
FREEDOM

Ephesians 1:6-7 (NLT) states:

> "So, we praise God for the glorious grace he has poured out on us who belong to his dear Son. He is so rich in kindness and grace that he purchased our freedom with the blood of his son and forgave our sins."

What a beautiful spiritual blessing. This freedom is so liberating: where we can come to the father, admit our faults, and know that we are forgiven. There is something, however, in the actual confession to another before God that really made it real for me.

As David states in Verses 1-2:

> "How happy and fulfilled are those whose rebellion has been forgiven. How blessed and relieved are those who have confessed their corruption to God! For he wipes their slates clean and removes hypocrisy from their hearts."

There is a freedom found in confession and forgiveness.

Since having lived through these five seasons for a period of my life that was very painful, I have come out the other side with a greater love for God, a deeper awareness of sin, a need to acknowledge the importance of confession and forgiveness, and a better understanding of freedom.

So, lets revisit the question I asked at the beginning:

Do you need to confess any sin that is holding you back from an increasing interpersonal relationship with God, which is preventing you from living in the full freedom of Christ?

Jot, draw, write, talk about it with God.

Loving Father,

We all go through these five seasons of sin, spiritual drought, surrender, forgiveness and freedom at some stage in life.

If we are in the season of sin, help us to recognise what it is on our heart that is keeping us from an intimate relationship with you.

If we are in a season of spiritual dryness, let your word soak through to our core and let us not give up faith.

If we are in a season of surrender, let us come forth with open hearts and open minds to receive your life-giving love.

If we are in a season of forgiveness, allow our hearts to be softened so that you can help us forgive others who have wronged us. Allow us also to receive your forgiveness for ourselves so that our relationship with you can be restored.

And if we are in a season of freedom, allow us to bask in the beautiful spiritual blessing you have bestowed upon us. Amen.

Love God, Love Others in Reality

Do you wear your heart on your sleeve?
Has your love for another been rejected?
Have you ever been insulted for loving?
Have you ever felt the deep love, joy and intimacy of another?

These are some confronting questions. What do you think of them?

During our lifetime, we all experience the reality of suffering because of love, and the immense joy because of love. Jesus experienced both suffering and joy. The deep, immense, intimate joy of knowing his father – a love so deep that it is unexplainable.

> *"You have entrusted me with all that you are and all that you have.*
> *No one fully and intimately knows the Son except the Father. And*
> *no one intimately and fully knows the Father except the Son. But*
> *the Son is able to unveil the Father to anyone he chooses."*
> *Matthew 11:27 TPT*

Jesus also had the ultimate suffering for love: his horrific, yet humble death on the cross for humanity. He was rejected, despised and insulted…

> *"They stripped him and put a scarlet robe on Him [as a king's*
> *robe.] And after twisting together a crown of thorns, they put*
> *it on His head, and put a reed in His right has [as a sceptre].*
> *Kneeling before Him, they ridiculed Him saying, "Hail*
> *(rejoice), King of the Jews!" They spat on Him, and took the*
> *reed and struck Him repeatedly on the head. After they finished*

ridiculing Him, they stripped Him of the scarlet robe and put His own clothes Him, and led Him away to crucify Him."
Matthew 27:28-31 AMP

Nothing can compare to the love that Jesus and our Heavenly Father have for us. This poses the question for me: How do I show love to others, and how do I show love to God?

Take a minute to think about these questions. Do you show love to others through words of encouragement and affirmation? Maybe hospitality or a joke? Intentional time with others listening, accepting and just being? Showing gratitude and saying 'thank you' often. Learning forgiveness.

Helping others at work, in the home, or volunteering?

How do you show your love to God? Prayer, worship, going to church, praise during the storms, then thankfulness for being pulled through, reading scripture or devotionals, taking in nature, being still with him?

Micah 6:8 NLT states

> *"No, O people, the Lord has told you what is good and this is what he requires of you: to do what is right, to love mercy and walk humbly with your God."*

This scripture is an important teaching … it expresses what is means to live with God, within the world.

Take a moment now to chat and jot with God. Ask him to open you up to this scripture within reality of your life – to do what is right, to love mercy and to walk humbly with God.

Hunger for God...Does it lead to peace for brokenness?

"The Lord helps the fallen and lifts those bent beneath their loads. The eyes of all look to you in hope; you give them their food as they need it.

When you open your hand, you satisfy the hunger and thirst of every living thing. The Lord is righteous in everything he does; he is filled with kindness.

The Lord is close to all who call on him, yes to all who call on him in truth.

He grants the desires of those who fear him; he hears their cries for help and rescues them."
Psalm 145:14-19 NLT

What really satisfies the hunger and longing in your soul? Is it the last Tim Tam in the packet? I've done that many times and it just makes me feel sick. Is it the last glass of wine, an empty bottle staring at you, your head a little dazed? I've done that too, and nope, it does nothing for me except make me feel sorry for myself and more depressed. Is it playing video games, being obsessed with sport, smoking, or being engulfed in Netflix or DVDs? Being with family and friends, always being busy and never being still…What really satisfies the hunger and longing in our soul?

What is it that deep down really wants to make you be alive, despite everything going on in your sphere of the world – the good, the bad and the ugly aspects of your life."

For me, the answer is God. I desire him, I am desperate for him. I thirst for him, I love him and I want more of him everyday because I need God immensely to help bring peace to my brokenness.

From a young age, I was always aware of God. However, I never recognised his magnitude and how much he loves me until I attempted suicide. I'll touch on that a bit later.

I grew up in an alcoholic home. My dad was a severe alcoholic and at times he did some horrible things. I was always walking on eggshells, wanting his love and approval. We had a love/hate relationship that was broken on the day he died.

I went to a Catholic primary school and high school. I made my First Holy Communion in year 3 and my Confirmation in year 6. I was also an alter girl and just loved church. The green and black speckled carpet, the statues of Jesus, the paintings on the walls, the organ up the back and the hard-wooden pews. It was a safe place, and I could feel a presence around me, which brought both a smile to my lips and tears to my eyes. However, as the years went by, I was beginning to break. I was beginning to fracture as cracks started appearing because I could not cope with turning into a teenager and I had no one to talk to. I felt empty and numb. I was deeply longing for 'something', but did not know what that 'something' was.

At age 15 in high school, things changed. The crack in my heart became deeper and I became cold. My nanna died the night before my 15th birthday, I was sexually assaulted, and my father's alcoholism was a roaring monster. At age 15 I started to self-harm, mainly cutting, and I started sniffing inhalants and drinking. At age 15 I started getting anorexic and wrote my first suicidal letter.

I was lost, hurt and angry. I would go to the Chapel at lunch times and scream to God in my head, Where are you? What the hell are you doing? I prayed the Psalm 18:6 NLT and hoped that he heard me everyday:

> *"But in my distress I cried out to the Lord; yes, I prayed to my God for help. He heard me from his sanctuary; my cry to him reached his ears."*

But, to my dismay, things got worse. By age 18, I was anorexic and weighed 40kg. My self-harm was horrendous, but it was the only way I could cope and keep myself alive. I hid it from my family and friends well. I also started having psychotic episodes, where I would hear voices, have delusional thoughts and see things that weren't really there. At some point I ended up in detox due to my drinking. That was eye opening and it was there that I swore that I would never be like my father.

Everyone thought I was a rebellious teenager because I was so moody - happy, talkative, sparkling, chirpy and laughing one minute – sad, crying, depressed, tired, anxious and grumpy the next. Eventually mum found out about the self-harm and whisked me away to the GP, then a psychiatrist, then the Black Dog Institute in Sydney, where I was diagnosed with Bipolar 1 Mood Disorder and severe anxiety. Well, what a relief that was for me because now it meant that we could do something to help make me better. That was my plan, anyway.

Mum and dad soon got divorced. I told the priest of the church I'd been attending since I was a child what my diagnosis was and his reply was, "People with a mental illness are a burden to society." I left that church gutted and did not enter another for many years - not until I was 33 years old.

However, I was still hungry and thirsty for God. I loved him. I needed him to love me. I needed an answer to the mess of my life. I needed healing for my brokenness. I often read the story of Jesus and the Samaritan woman:

> *"Jesus answered her, "Everyone who drinks this water will be thirsty again, but whoever drinks the water that I give him will never be thirsty again. But the water that I give him will become in him a spring of water (satisfying his thirst for God) welling up (continually flowing, bubbling within him) to eternal life."*
> *John 4:13-14 AMP*

Well, that was just what I wanted – a fountain of the Holy Spirit inside me, flooding me with peace and love.

But the brokenness did not stop there. I had countless admissions to psychiatric units, both public and private. I had medication trials that where relentless as I had so many allergic reactions. In my 20's I had ECT - Electro Convulsive Therapy - for a severe depressive episode. ECT is a form of treatment where you go under a general anaesthetic. A strap is placed on your forehead and tiny electrodes are placed on your head, which are hooked up to a machine with leads that give the electrical shock/current. Your body goes through a tiny seizure – just so your toes wiggle. It is performed three times a week for up to 10 weeks. At that stage, in my 20s, which was the early 2000s, I had ECT on both sides of my brain. I lost a lot of memory, which still has not come back to this day.

Then, there was a glimmer of sunshine. Although the ECT did not help a great deal, I did meet a man in 2005. We dated for many years, then got married. There were elements of abuse in the relationship, and it got to the point that the relationship became toxic, so I decided to leave the marriage in 2015. I left in the middle of the night, in my PJ's with my dog. I was homeless for 12 months. I mostly stayed with my mum and stepdad, living out of my suitcase. It was a taxing time for us all. This was when I started going back to church. In hindsight, this was all a blessing. New friends, a church family was awaiting me.

In November 2015, my father died a horrific death due to his alcoholism. His last breath was projectile bile all over me. I believe God placed me to be an instrument of his peace for my father. It was in his dying moments that I saw my dad and myself in all our human brokenness. There was a healing, a peace, and an anointing over our relationship which is difficult to explain. However, I know that God was at work, and that my dad is now in heaven free of his demons, and that he smiles down on me every day, in gratitude for being by his side when I could have easily walked away.

March 2016 rolls around and my pop passes away. I am in the psych unit so unable to attend the funeral. I had so much anger.

In September 2016, I had to have a hysterectomy – more grief, loss, anger and brokenness. A heart freezing over. September of that year also granted me a house for my little dog and I, which was a real blessing and answer to prayer.

In February 2017, I had another round of ECT for another severe depressive episode. I was also diagnosed with complex PTSD, along with the bipolar 1 and anxiety. I was gutted. My heart was beating cold in a rib cage that was barely moving as breathing hurt. Severed, my heart and soul were ripped in two and I was over powered by depression, pain and deep loss.

Yet, I still had this hunger for God.
Was I angry at God for how my life had turned out? YES
Was I complaining and whinging to God about how awful things were? YES
Was I swearing and cursing and letting it rip? YES
Do you think God could handle all that? Of course, he did!!

I had to rant and rave, scream and cry, yell and get mad because that's how I drew close to God. He knew my pain, yet I also knew there would be a time when I could rejoice.

Just like Habakkuk 3:17-18 (NIV) states:

> *"Though the fig tree does not bud and there are no grapes on the vines,*
> *though the olive crop fails and the fields produce no food,*
> *though there are no sheep in the pen and no cattle in the stalls,*
> *yet I will rejoice in the Lord,*
> *I will be joyful in God my Savior"*

During 2017-2018, my love for the Lord grew so much. I had found a family and was beginning to settle into church community. My church family are so loving, accepting, real and gentle. This was something I had not experienced before, and found quite hard to accept. But it was in 2017 when I did the Walk to Emmaus the question I've been holding on to for so long: *Hunger for God... does it lead to peace for brokenness?* was finally beginning to be answered.

My frozen heart. My chipped, fractured, broken, severed heart was slowly starting to be glued back together by God's love. Psalm 139 brought this home for me – because God knows all about me. God's love is continually changing me. I need to let God love me and not push him away. I need to be vulnerable before him. I do not need to do anything to get God's love. For years, I compared my earthly father to my Heavenly Father. God loves me, no matter what. I do not need his approval. There is head knowledge of this and heart knowledge of this. I think you need to have both. I know sometimes when I am unwell, this knowledge is confused with the illness and I need my church family to remind me of who I am – a beloved child of God.

In April 2019, I had an attempt on my life while being an inpatient at a mental health facility. It was a very dark, bleak, distressing time for me, and others. It felt as though I was rotten, that somewhere deep-seeded in me there is a rainforest with tree roots so deeply embedded into the ground that my heart and mind had been taken over by nothingness, hopelessness and lack of purpose. The vines in the rainforest wrapped around my ankles, making me stuck, and they covered my mind in a tangle of negativity, self-hate, numbness and being suicidal. I was psychotic, self-harming and was determined to die…to be hit by the cars and busses on the road as I ran around.

Somehow, a nurse took me to the Chapel at Calvary Hospital and I was able to talk to him, talk to God, then spend time with pastoral care. It was my chat with the pastoral care lady that really grounded me. We talked about the wounded healer – how Jesus weeps with you. That he suffered physically in human form so that we can hide in his wounds for healing. We prayed and cried together. Then I started thinking again: you are sick, this is an illness, this is not you, you are a beloved child of God. I reflected on the rainforest – damp with thick roots and vines holding me captive in the dark, yet it could be a place of new growth if I let God in and allow acceptance of God's love for me, and the communities love for me, even though I am so sick.

This was a turning point; light was peeping into the darkness of my suicidal mind and God was telling me to rest a while in Jesus' wounds. I took comfort in Romans 8:16 TPT:

> *"For the Holy Spirit makes God's fatherhood real to us as he whispers into our inner most being 'You are God's beloved child."*
> *So, does hunger for God lead to peace for brokenness?*
> *Does God satisfy the hunger and longing in your soul?*

What is it that deep down really wants you to be alive, despite everything going on in your sphere of the world?

My answer with my life experiences is YES, hunger for God does lead to peace for brokenness.

Yes, God satisfies the hunger and longing in my soul, and yes, without God, even though I still get very sick and become suicidal at times, life would not be worth living because God has been so faithful to me and there would be no hope. God is my refuge and my strength. He is my healer, my protector, my sunrise of a morning, my starlight at night. He is all I need. He blesses me every day, and every day I am hungry, needing to surrender and be vulnerable before him so I can receive that peace for brokenness. It does not always come easy, and yes, I struggle. However God knows that, and that is okay, because after all, we are his beloved children.

> *"I am passionately in love with God because he listens to me. He hears my prayers and answers them. As long as I live I'll keep praying to him, for he stoops down to listen to my hearts cry. Death once stared me in the face, and I was close to slipping into its dark shadows. I was terrified and over come with sorrow. I cried out to the Lord "God, come and save me!" He was so kind and gracious to me. Because of his passion toward me he made everything right and restored me. So, I've learned from my experiences that God protects the childlike and humble ones. For I was broken and brought low, but he answered me and came to my rescue! Now I can say to myself and all "Relax and rest, be confident and serene, for the Lord rewards fully those who simply trust in him.""*
> *Psalm 116:1-7 TPT*

Jottings

Are you hungry for God?
Express this hunger through a word, a
drawing, a prayer or scripture.

Explaining Faith

During a stay at a mental health unit that was a long way from my home town, I found myself fully reliant on God. In an unfamiliar setting, with people I did not know, I found myself acting out my faith and speaking to believers and unbelievers alike.

Now, I am not a ram-it-down-your-throat type of person. Far from it. I am shy, quiet, reserved. I like to demonstrate my faith through my values and actions. Yes, talking about faith is pivotal as well. However, at times I feel I can choke.

On this particular day, I did not choke.

I was in the art room one afternoon and I had a long conversation with a volunteer artist, a man who said he was an atheist. We were talking about art in the time of Jesus. The gentleman was doing an online course in Italy and was telling me about a piece at The Last Supper.

As he described, 'All of the disciples are gathered with Jesus at the table, and one man has a dagger behind his back.' The volunteer artist thought this man was angry and was going to kill someone. At the same time the gentleman was conflicted in his thoughts because he thought that the disciples and Jesus were all loving, caring people. The gentleman could not figure out the dagger.

I explained to this man that in the Bible, when the cock crowed three times, Peter denied Jesus, so the dagger could represent a 'stab in the back', or betrayal. I was then surprised to see his facial reaction – it was like he had a lightbulb moment and said, 'that makes sense.'

It was a great conversation. God placed me in the right situation to explain to this man a little about what I believe and help him understand a possible answer to his question.

Another person I spoke to daily was a nurse who administrated the TMS (Transcranial Brain Magnetic Stimulation). The nurse asked me a very difficult question: 'Why do you think some people in their lives experience more trauma than others?'

How on earth does someone answer that? I asked God for guidance and replied to the nurse, 'I don't have an answer to that question, but what I do know is that no matter what I go through, and how much I dislike it, it is being used for God's glory. Is this very difficult to see and understand at times – yes, very much so. However, I know that God has it all planned, as he has got me in the palm of his hand, and I trust him.'

At the end of the TMS session, the nurse said to me, 'Anita, you have left me with a lot to think about. Thank you.'

In both circumstances, God placed me with people who had questions. I was able to ask God for guidance in trying to answer them, and through His Spirit, I was able to share my faith.

Each person was intrigued about a particular question: the artist and his conflicted thoughts about the disciples, and the nurse wanting to know life's biggest question... why do some people suffer more than others? My explanation of these questions left the listener with something to think about, allowing God to tap on their heart and invite them to search for more.

And, that's what I think one element of trying to explain faith is about – leaving your listener with a thought or question that intrigues them, then letting God go to work and knock on their heart, so as to welcome them and explore more.

> *"Instruct and teach the people all I've taught you. And don't be intimated by those who are older than you; simply be the example they need to see by being faithful and true in all that you do. Speak the truth and live a life of purity and authentic love, as you remain strong in your faith."*
> *1 Timothy 4:11-12 TPT*

Jottings

How do you act out your faith?

Have you ever choked when trying to explain your faith to someone? What did you do?

Have you ever had an experience where explaining faith was easy and welcomed?

What's in your House?

My little Hugo was a cheerful soul at my feet and a delight in my heart. He brought great joy, safety and companionship to my life and within my home.

I have a plaque that sits on my bookshelf. It reads *A house is not a home without Paw Prints*. I brought it when I was in a mental health unit a long way from home town. I was missing Hugo immensely. This plaque allowed me to really think about Hugo ... what he means to me, all the trials and obstacles we have shared and overcome together.

The plaque has great significance, not only as a cute decoration, but as a representation of my heart as a house for God, and my heart is not a home without His Spirit.

Intellectually I know this, yet sometimes my house, the sacred place of intimate relationship with God, is overtaken with pain, unforgiveness, anger and anxiety. This leaves little room for the joy of His Spirit in the home of my heart. It is during these times that my heart, a blessed place, needs to be surrendered ... an open-door welcoming God in to do a thorough clean.

Once cleaned, I come to realise again that my home is a sacred place where I come to be in communion with God. It is he who provides joy, safety and companionship. Without His Spirit, my heart, 'the house where his lives', is not a home.

> *"Have you forgotten that your body is now the sacred temple of the Spirit of Holiness who lives in you? You don't belong to yourself any longer, for the gift of God, the Holy Spirit lives inside your sanctuary." 1 Corinthians 6:19 TPT*

Jottings

Think about your heart as a home for God and how your heart is not a home without His Spirit. What words, reflections or creative responses do you have?

Do you have anything in your home, the place of intimate relationship with God, that needs cleaning out? Invite God into this place for a thorough clean.

What does the Holy Spirit provide for you in the home of your heart – joy, peace, comfort etc?

Father,

Thank you for paw prints in our homes that bring mischief, cheer and love – whether that be dogs, cats, birds or any other creature you created. More importantly, though, thank you for making your home in our hearts where we experience deep joy, hope, unfailing love, forgiveness, companionship and safety. A place where intimacy is deep and the Spirit is alive. Amen.

Poetry

Try and write a poem about how you are feeling right now. There is no right or wrong way.

The Book of Psalms is a book of poetry expressing so many human emotions – anger, frustration, praise, thanksgiving, joy, hope love. Have a read and see if you can write a poem explaining your feelings and relationship with God.

_____

_____

_____

_____

_____

_____

_____

Beautifully Cracked

Beautifully cracked,
I find myself hiding in your wounds.
My source of strength,
You make me sure footed as a deer on a mountain top.

Beautifully cracked,
Damaged,
I find myself being repaired by your grace.
Your death on the cross,
My source of healing.

Beautifully cracked,
Split,
But not separate from you.
The length, depth and width of your love
Is beyond my comprehension.

I am beautifully cracked,
And you are holding me together.
Even though I feel broken,
You will not allow me to fully break.

Cracks in my soul,
Allow for a deep intimate relationship with you…
Gentle healing taking place,
One crack at a time…

I am beautifully cracked and tenderly held together.

"You will be the inner strength of all your people, the mighty protector of all, the saving strength for all your anointed ones."
Psalm 28:8 TPT

From Your Feet

I look at you,
On that Cross.
I see … in eyes of faith.
I feel … in a heart of grace.
I love … enormously.

We collide in a moment,
Immersed in the Fathers love,
And I know this is where I belong.

Kissing your feet,
At the foot of the Cross
Is where transformation begins.

Healing:

New life sprouts forth
From your feet.
A rose,
A sweet scent,
Delicate, colourful;
A reminder of your promises of restoration.

And I look at you on that Cross,
I see … in eyes of growth.
I feel … in my heart, joy, gratitude
And I love … with an everlasting love.

"Then you will be empowered to discover what every holy one experiences – the great magnitude of the astonishing love of Christ in all its dimensions. How deeply intimate and far-reaching is his love! Endless love beyond measurement that transcends our understanding – this extravagant love pours into you until you are filled to overflowing with the fullness of God!"
Ephesians 3:18-19 TPT

How I Love You

Deep,
I'm crying
With an ache in my heart.
Not one of sorrow or pain,
But an ache to go deeper;
To know you more.

Crying out
Hand stretched high in surrender
I seek you:
'Come Holy Spirit,'
I cry with tears of joy
'Fill me up to overflow.'

Meet me
In this secret place
Where our hearts collide …
A passion for each other
A love so deep,
It astounds me.

Unexplainable:

Oh, how I love you!

"God – you're my God! I can't get enough of you!
I've worked up such a hunger and thirst for God, travelling across
weary deserts.
So here I am in the place of worship, eyes open, drinking in your
strength and glory. In your generous love I am really living at last!
My lips brim praises like fountains. I bless you every time I take
a breath;
My arms wave like banners of praise to you."
Psalm 63:1-4 MSG

Made Pure as Gold

Broken,
My heart wears a scar.
That scar is precious.
It is lived experience.
A trial of suffering:
Pain, sadness, grief and loss.
An example of endurance.

With this scar comes the opportunity for healing if I am open;
A refining power from Gods own heart …
A burning away of the pain,
Turning iron into silver and gold,
Impurities melted away.

With needle and thread,
My heart is tenderly stitched.

I am refined,
The stitches dissolve into the scars of Jesus' hands, feet and side …

And I am left washed,
I am drenched in blood
And made pure as gold.

> *"In the same way that gold and silver are refined by fire,
> the Lord purifies your heart by the tests and trials of life."*
> *Proverbs 17:3 TPT*

My Anchor

The storm is raging inside of me:
I'm in the middle of the ocean,
Wind, lightning, hail and rain.
Waves of cold salty water are crashing over me.

My anxiety is high.
My heart is pounding in my chest.
I am saturated with fear.
The grip of depression
Has taken me captive,
And all I see is darkness.

I call out your name …
'Jesus, come and help me!'
And with in an instant
A loud voice in a clap of thunder
Tells me to throw the anchor overboard.

I make my way to the hull of the ship.
There I see the anchor.
It is covered in fresh, brightly coloured flowers,
An olive branch of peace and hope.
I pause for a second, puzzled …
Then another wave crashes over me.

With all my might,
I throw the anchor overboard,
And within an instant
The storm inside of me starts to settle.

Then, it finally makes sense,
As the rays of sun gently warm my heart
And blue skies replace the dark.

The storm inside has settled,
I have hope and peace.
Jesus is my anchor.
With him I am grounded,
And can withstand the rough seas.

> *"The voice of the LORD is heard on the seas; the glorious God thunders, and his voice echoes over the ocean. The voice of the LORD is heard in all its might and majesty."*
> *Psalm 29:3-4 GNT*

Warrior

Jesus,
You've made me a warrior.
A fighter for the truth despite at times the negativity in my head.
A brave woman who struggles and falls to her knees,
Yet dusts off the dirt and gets back to her feet to proclaim your goodness.
A courageous lady,
With a spirit of confidence, not a spirit of fear.

Jesus,
You've made me a warrior.
Strong in faith.
Strong in prayer.
Strong in love for you.

Jesus,
You've made me a warrior.
To continue on, each day afresh in the grace of God.
To count my blessings no matter my circumstances.
To surrender before the Cross.
To be infused with your Holy Spirit.
To have an empowering relationship with you.

Jesus,
You've made me a warrior.
A person who fights the good fight,
Armed with your heavenly protection as my shield,
Your love as my breast plate,

Your wisdom as my helmet
And embedded faith as my sword.

Jesus,
You've made me a warrior.

> *"Now my beloved ones, I have saved these most important truths*
> *for last: Be supernaturally infused with strength through your life-*
> *union with the Lord Jesus. Stand victorious with the force of his*
> *explosive power flowing in and through you."*
> *Ephesians 6:10 TPT*

The Journey of Friendship

People,
Journeying through life
To a place of love, belonging and forgiveness.
Transforming each other,
They bring truth and light into the darker spots of our lives.
Challenging times allow for dedication, loyalty and a nest of acceptance
and love where we can rest and be restored.
When our hearts are nourished,
And we begin to fly again,
Friends ignite our passion and identity,
Allowing our inner beauty to shine.

Protective barriers drop,
When one feels safe and at ease with another ...
Real belly laughter takes place in joyous times,
Currents of tears are wiped with a tissue when things are bad.
Understanding is precious,
Listening is vital,
Jokes make the journey lighter,
A hug expresses love and care.

A friend awakens the spirit,
Teaches us vulnerability and trust.
They walk beside you,
Catching you when you trip and graze your knee,
They nurture.

Friendships are vital,
Connections are deep,
Smiles warm the heart,
And appreciation is important to show.

A friend is a gift from God,
Someone special.
A messenger brought into your life
To teach you things about yourself.
To bring companionship, adventure, fun and hope.

Friends,
People journeying through life together -
People connecting,
Accepting,
Laughing, crying
Loving, belonging, forgiving each other ...
The greatness of God at work in each person's life,
Shining through the spirit of one person to the next.

> *"The heartfelt counsel of a friend is as sweet as perfume and insence."*
> *Proverbs 27:9 NLT*

The Dark Side, Broken by Light

A splintered back,
On a rugged wooden cross
Nails hammered deep,
A pierced side
Thorns crushed on your head,
Beads of sweat
Blood.

Dark black clouds surround you
Rusty chains envelope you
Heavy ... you take on the sin of the world.

The clouds keep brewing,
Darkness covers the land
"My God, My God, why have you abandoned me?"
It is finished.

His head hangs,
The chains snap and gather at the foot of His cross ...
The power, the victory has been won ...

The shadow of death, the dark side has been broken by His light.

A pure glow surrounds the cross,
A shining radiance now covers the whole land.

Hearts are ignited ...
Ablaze with freedom and love,

For the Son of God died to encompass our
hearts with a deep affectionate love-

Grace: love and mercy gently colliding just as God wants us to have it …
Freely given because we are his children.

> *"His light broke through the darkness and led us out in freedom*
> *from deaths dark shadow, and snapped every one of our chains."*
> *Psalm 107:14 TPT*

Precious Healing Tears

Tapping on my heart
'Anita let me in,'
'Yes Lord,' I said courageously
Awaiting the healing process to begin.

'It's been a long time Lord ... all this hurt and anger needs to go,'
So God filled my eyes with tears,
And abundantly they flowed.

The colours of blue, yellow, orange and pink
Stream down my cheeks ...
Each tear drop life giving
Surrounded by righteousness,
And a gold band of peace.

Blue tears bring calm,
Washing away anger, hurt and pain,
Cleansing me from my sin,
Blessing others,
And giving me freedom.

Yellow tears bring the light to dispel the darkness,
And the truth of your word to soak into my heart and mind.
This reminds me that you ae my anchor,
And your love for me is unconditional and kind.

Orange tears bring
The hope and strength I find in you …
A gentle reminder
That surrender is a constant thing I need to do.

Pink tears bring
The new found joy that makes my heart,
Skip with a beat of delight;
Knowing that you Jesus
Are my Savior,
And my battles you will fight.

'Thank you Lord for these precious healing tears,' I gratefully say to God …
'Anita my child, in my bottle they are all stored.'

> *"You've kept track of all my wandering and weeping. You've stored*
> *my many tears in your bottle. Not one will be lost. For they are all*
> *recorded in your book of remberance."*
> *Psalm 56:8 TPT*

Drink from the Cup

To seek
To find
A love so divine,
Is to drink from the cup
Of Jesus' hand.

Living water,
Invitations to all
Quenches thirst;
For the life of love
Jesus planned
Is the drink form the cup,
Of His nailed scarred hand.

Sparkling new life,
The water redeems,
As one sips the cup
And transformation begins …

Let the living water soothe you,
Let it come and add zest to your life;
For to drink from the cup
Is to rest assured
That Jesus is for you,
And His promises bring new life.

"Soon a Samartian woman came to draw water, and Jesus said to her, "Please give me a drink." He was alone at the time because his disciples had gone into the village to buy some food. The woman was surprised, for Jews refuse to have anything to do with Samaritans. She said to Jesus, "You are a Jew, and I am a Samaritan woman. Why are you asking me for a drink?" Jesus replied, "If only you knew the gift God has for you, and who you are speaking to, you would ask me, and I would give you living water.""

John 4:7-10 NLT

The Thistle

There was a hole in his hand,
And outstretched in his palm was a thistle -
Pointy, sharp, brown and blood stained.

'I love you this much'…
He whispered in my ear,
And laid his hand on my heart.

'Will you receive this love?'
The man gently asks …
The thistle sharp,
Yet full of compassion is pushed against my heart.

I look him in the eye
Soft and warm,
'Yes' I reply.

He gently says,
'This is not love as you know it on earth -
It is the love of the Father,
Sent through me,
With nails and thorns to set you free.'

He goes on to say,
'This love is delightful
And breaks all chains
If you surrender all to me each day.'

'This is easier said than done' he says,
'And I know there will be times
When you feel distant and go astray
But,
Know that the hole and thistle in my hand
Is my divine love for you.
It is planted in your heart,
And day by day,
This love will see you through.'

A message of encouragement from Anita

Dear friends,

I encourage you to always remember that God's gift to you is love; love that is powerful and able to overcome every obstacle. Love that makes you strong in your weakness. Love that envelopes you and is wrapped around you so tightly that all you can do is breathe in this love.

I want to encourage you to keep praying, in all seasons.

I want you to know that although you have been tested, in many different ways, in many different seasons, the Lord your God has been with you.

I want to encourage you to remember the cross and what it stands for – immense love, renewal, new life, transformation, forgiveness, surrender.

What I have to say to you is GOD LOVES YOU.

Blessings,
Anita.